Boy

My lady story

Boy

I eat less. Less. I want less. I want less skin, fat, body. Breasts. Chicken. Skinny. Love.

A boy. I'd prefer to be –

A boy.

I cry.

I see myself, others.

Art.

Effort

"Who will love you?
Who will fight?
Who will fall far behind?"

Bon Iver

Fly

I feel angry. Furious.

My parents, family. Friends.

Being boyish, no longer girly, allows me to feel my feelings. Express myself. Fully.

Fuck you, guys. Fuck you. All.

Wall

I'm feeling so much, I never felt before.

Whore.

Heart

Break.

Sorry

It is not just, sadness. Tears. Trying out, different stories.

It is truth.

Loss

I lost my baby. Boy.

And my friend.

Others

Mothers.

Grief

A funeral.

For myself, my baby.

Boy.

Thief

Loss, grief. Tears, joy. Toy.

Boy.

Gender

My cat.

Cries, mourns, bites.

I kick. Her. Him. I'm not sure why.

All this. Anger. I tap, try, out. Otra ves. All this. Anger.

My Sponsee. Calls.

I'm so. Fucking.

Angry.

Gay

The past is no longer true.

None of it. Life changes, day by day.

I'm furious. It's not, okay.

I'm sorry. Please forgive me. I love you. Thank you.

Too.

Bye

I cry. Some, times, cut, sharp. Knives.

Food. Purge, puke. People bring me plates, I get sick, do not eat. Everything. Little. Throw. Away.

Left-over food.

Fiction.

Fantasy

"I don't care, go on and tear me apart
I don't care if you do ooh ooh
'Cause in a sky, 'cause in a sky full of stars
I think I saw you
'Cause you're a sky, you're a sky full of stars
Such a heavenly view
You're such a heavenly view"

Coldplay

Truly

Listen. Just try to listen. One thing, at a time. Listen to your Sponsee. It's your fucking job.

Universe. All the stars, planets, forms of matter. 10 billion light years old.

Peace. A stress free state, security. No fighting or war. Everything coexisting in perfect harmony. Freedom.

Serenity. The state or quality of being serene, calm, tranquil.

Time. The –

Slip

Posture. The posture of someone, standing, sitting.

Discipline. The practicing of –

Prayer. A prayer is –

Love. A very strong feeling of affection towards someone.

Heart

Home.

I stay. Away.

I can't, I say. Go home.

People don't recognize me. Anymore. Whore.

Chore. Until I do. Go home. They say boy, girl. Where have you been?

Alive, I say. Strive.

Here.

Queer

I've been here. All along, I say.

Only you don't believe me. Pray.

You say I lie. Pretend. To be someone, I'm not.

I forgot. Who I am, what I used, to be doing. For a living. Life.

Wife.

Worry

And so I worry. A lot.

Will I ever –

Be me. Free. Forever.

Fight

Lights go out.

Night.

Copy

I copy. You.

What you did.

To me.

To others. Mothers.

It is not fair.

Flair

A library.

My fantasy.

Art.

Circles

Celibacy.

Celebrity.

Success

Story.

Angry

Hate. Intense hostility.

Sponsee continues.

Aversion, driven by fear, anxiety. Anger.

Injury.

Extreme dislike, disgust. Intense revulsion.

"What is coping", she asks.

I reply, shortly. "It's dealing with. Negativity".

People, feelings. Emotions.

"I'm coping with you". I think, but do not say, it, out loud.

Shout

Fuck it. I'm not your mom. Adult. Child.

I'm so pissed off. Angry. Furious.

Fuck it. Why do I feel this way? I don't recognize myself. Anymore.

Liquor

My writing is rubbish.

Is it?

I'll distill what's necessary, later on.

In life.

AA

A beach. Holiday. Camp.

Yoga.

Joy.

Sutra

But I did, slip. And now I feel lost, confused. Broken.

And I must, continue.

And my Sponsee, too. She slipped. After I slipped.

Karma.

Colorful

Queer. Here, in Cusco. Peru.

Nature

I felt it first. At my cat. Anger, rage. Fury. Now I feel it suddenly. Everywhere.

There.

Wisdom

A wild, child. Jungle, nature.

Art.

Sponsee continues.

Pride.

A feeling of relief, sensation. Pleasure, satisfaction.

Dignity.

Stories

"I feel proud", Sponsee says. "Of completing these questions, one by one. I hated doing it, but now I've done it, I feel so much better. Lighter."

"I feel relieved."

"Congratulations", I say.

Pride

My pride is different. It's not just proud. It's pride.

Dictionary

We continue going. Few minutes, more.

Resentment. "Anger, for doing wrong. Insult".

Injury. "Jealousy. Rivalry".

"A person enjoying success, over another. Person".

Play.

And she tells me, a story. Ex-boyfriend. Hatred. Jealousy.

"It's time", I say. "I need to go".

Few more words. I try to, listen carefully.

Writing. "The process of using symbols, letters of the alphabet".

Reading. "The process of –"

She lost me. I'm gone.

"I'm sorry", I say. I –

Cry

"Can I share"? I ask.

"Yes", she says, "please do so".

"I felt so angry", I say, all morning. "At you, my cat, my parents. Everyone".

"And now I see, it's me. No one else, but me. And it's not just, anger. It's sadness, confusion. Fear. I'm terrified. Of letting go, what was. My identity. I feel so boyish, lately. A boy. I hate it. Love it. I'm not sure what to do with it. But I can't change it, really.

I can't".

"Thank you", she says. "For sharing".

And I love her, all of a sudden. I feel calm. Better. Bright.

A boy.

Night.

Light

After calling, I go to Reiki. I cry. My eyes. Out.

"You're broken", Vento says.

Into two.

Stars

"Call it magic, call it true
I call it magic when I'm with you
And I just got broken, broken into two
Still I call it magic, when I'm next to you"

Coldplay

Cusco

It's cold. I turn on my heater, gas, fire. Warm.

Few minutes later, I'm hot. Kitty comes, out. Into my chest, seat, belt. Beauty.

He's beautiful. It's a boy.

So why do I hate him so?

Love

How to love, fully, truly, unconditionally.

Not refuse, resist, retract. Act.

But simply let, love, be. Breathe.

Gently, heavily. Art.

Heart.

And if it's difficult, let it be. Difficult. It's okay.

Stay.

Try your best. Every day.

Pray.

Love each other nonetheless. Each other.

Mother.

Child.

Clarity

"And if you were to ask me
After all that we've been through
Still believe in magic?
Well yes, I do

Oh yes, I do
Oh yes, I do
Oh yes, I do
Of course I do"

Coldplay

Curious

Zoë. My best.

Friend.

Cusco

"We're going out", she says. "Do you join"?

I say yes. And then no.

I cancel. And then go.

To bed.

Cars

"It's been a long day without you my friend
And I'll tell you all about it when I see you again
We've come a long way from where we began
Oh I'll tell you all about it when I see you again
When I see you again"

Wiz Khalifa

Chicago

I'll visit you one day, I say.

Gay.

Diner

"Let's go for pizza, lady."

Baby.

Talk

Softly, you smile.

Often.

My

My hair, short.

I play with what's left, of my sweater.

Weather. I say, it's time to go. Often.

Only I don't, go. I stay.

Next to you, close. By.

Circle

I write. Plenty.

Massive amounts of words, drip from my fingers.

Tips.

Work

A coffee shop. Finally.

I act upon my writing.

A different order.

Life.

Wifey

I no longer strive.

To do better, to be different. To be someone I'm not.

Yet.

Heart

A meeting. Online, SLAA.

For dummies.

I say hi, greet others. Mothers.

They make my day.

Say what?

Say hey.

Nama-stay.

Hurt

My body hurts. Aches, my heart.

Hips, hallelujah.

Home.

Body

They say, "let go".

Trauma, tension. Release.

Your anger, let go.

Money

Matters.

Art

I'm so done. Being different. A boy.

I'm so done.

Doing.

Stay

"Still", my mom says.

"Why do you move so often?"

Gipsy

Generosity.

I decide to stay. Longer.

Here.

Queer

And I ask, my Grandmother.

In my sleep.

"Why does it hurt so much?"

She replies, softly. Quietly.

"Because you're growing, baby".

It is not your fault. It just is. What it is.

Today.

Pray

God.

"I offer myself to Thee –

To build with me and to do with me as Thou wilt.

Amen".

Ayahuasca

In Ceremony, I receive. Answers.

To all of my questions.

One by one.

God

"Grant me. The serenity. To accept the things I cannot change, the courage. To change the things I can.

And the wisdom to know. The difference.

Thy will not mine, be done.

Amen".

Art

My eyes. Fill.

Tears.

Timing

Is it true?

I can't remember –

You.

Santa Marta

A massage, coconut, scrub. Cacao. Avocado. My body.

Tensed.

Hot.

Why do I try to be someone I'm not?

Any

More.

Whore

"Don't", I say. "Please don't."

I'm terrified. Afraid.

Again.

Brave

I eat fat, salt. Spicy food.

My body's changing. In every single way.

Gay.

Lover

"I close my eyes, only for a moment, and the moment's gone
All my dreams pass before my eyes, a curiosity
Dust in the wind
All they are is dust in the wind

Same old song, just a drop of water in an endless sea
All we do crumbles to the ground though we refuse to see
Dust in the wind
All we are is dust in the wind

Now, don't hang on, nothing lasts forever but the earth and
sky
It slips away
And all your money won't another minute buy
Dust in the wind

All we are is dust in the wind
All we are is dust in the wind
Dust in the wind
Everything is dust in the wind
Everything is dust in the wind"

Kansas

Hover

/'hɒvə/
verb

remain in one place in the air
"Army helicopters hovered overhead"

noun
an act of remaining in the air in one place
"keep the model in a stable hover"

Cover

I cover up.

My breasts, chest. Open, shirts.

Close.

Creation

Dose

My mom visits me.

"I might be gay".

"It's okay".

Nay

Only it's not. Okay.

Say, I'm sorry. Please forgive me. I love you.

Thank you.

Do

I do not tell you. Everything.

Only little.

Toy

I do not tell you I feel boyish. Not just boyish, *a boy.*

In every possible way.

Stay. Say.

It's okay.

Nay.

Gay

My body.

Hurts.

My hips, throat.

My sacrum.

I can't play. Pretend.

Anymore.

Whore

Hate.

Myself, others.

You.

Too

Vulnerability.

Shame.

Work

Twerk.

Trap

My temper. Anger.

Frustration.

Fear.

Ferocity

/fəˈrɒsɪti/
noun

the state or quality of being ferocious
"the ferocity of the storm caught them by surprise"

Fantasy.

My future.

Disney

Let it go.

Ice

Queen.

Cold.

Culture

Call me.

Maybe.

Baby

"Call me by my name."

My name.

Not yours.

                              Why

My way.

Gay.

People

Say boy, girl. Senorita.

Senor.

Silent

Ill.

Fever.

Santa Marta

Coco

"Ten decisions shape your life
You'll be aware of 5 about
7 ways to go through school
Either you're noticed or left out
7 ways to get ahead
7 reasons to drop out
When I said "I can see me in your eyes"
You said "I can see you in my bed"
That's not just friendship that's romance too
You like music we can dance to

Sit me down
Shut me up
I'll calm down
And I'll get along with you"

The Strokes, I'll Try Anything Once

Present

My life is now.

And so I go. Out.

All my life I've been hiding. Now I'm free.

Fall. Often.

Love.

In. Out. Others.

Stories.

Mothers

My ties get bigger.

Muscles

I get bigger.

Strong.

Wrong

A life. Long.

Love.

Song

Sweet.

Disposition.

Dust

Dreams.

Free

A library. Resort.

Playa.

People

Attention.

Moon

Full.

Swimming

Pool.

Pleasure

I meet you.

I miss you.

Airport

You say, I pray.

You don't believe in prayer.

Nay-sayer.

Player

Trio.

Time

Soon.

Coffee

Corazon

Del Mundo.

Lobster

A long day.

Wonderful way.

Gay

You're pretty, I say.

Bay

Every day.

Sister

Senorita.

"On that sunny day
Didn't know I'd meet
Such a beautiful girl
Walking down the street
Seen those bright brown eyes
With tears coming down
She deserves a crown
But where is it now

Mamma listen

Senorita, I feel for you
You deal with things, that you don't have to
He doesn't love ya, I can tell by his charm
But you could feel this real love
If you just lay in my

Running fast in my mind
Girl don't you slow it down
If we carry on this way
This thing might leave the ground
How would you like to fly?
That's how my queen should arrive
But you still deserve the crown
Or hasn't it been found?

Mamma listen"

God

A Course in Miracles, T-12.I.7:

> "Your interpretations of your brother's needs are your interpretation of yours.
>
> By giving help you are asking for it, and if you perceive but one need in yourself you will be healed.
>
> For you will recognize God's Answer as you want It to be, and if you want It in truth, It will be truly yours.
>
> Every appeal you answer in the Name of Christ brings the remembrance of your Father closer to your awareness.
>
> For the sake of your need, then, hear every call for help as what it is, so God can answer you".

Star

One day, I try to. Tell you.

I love you.

Too

Were we ready?

To go steady.

I guess –

Not.

Mercury

Yet.

Retrograde

/ˈrɛtrəgreɪd/

directed or moving backwards
"a retrograde flow"

reverting to an earlier and inferior condition
"to go back on the progress that has been made would be a
retrograde step"

(of amnesia) involving the period immediately preceding the causal
event

(of the order of something) reversed; inverse
"the retrograde form of these inscriptions"

Should

If only –

I could let go.

Of my should. I should –

Go.

Must

I did not.

Need to go but I left.

Nonetheless.

Movie

Must.

I follow my muse.

Writings.

Words

Why don't I put love first?

Thirst.

Art

When will I ever?

Never.

Say

Never.

Ever

"I love you always, forever
Near and far, closer together
Everywhere I will be with you
Every sin, I will do for you
I love you always, forever
Near and far, closer together
Everywhere I will be with you
Every sin, I will do for you"

Betty Who, Always Forever

Aim

/eɪm/

verb

a purpose or intention; a desired outcome.
"our primary aim is to achieve financial discipline"

the directing of a weapon or missile at a target.
"his aim was perfect"

Amen

Air.

Fresh.

Family

Four.

Children.

Car. Cruising.

Custody

Clarity.

Queen

Nike

Don't define, just do.

It.

What

And what if I don't? Do it?

You'll regret it. Forever.

Social

And so I must.

Trust.

Instagram

And so I post. A picture.

A boy, girl.

A not so sure yet. Of everything.

Anything. Can change, so quickly. Life. In a minute.

Second. Star.

I'm feeling far. Better. Stronger, lighter. Fitter.

Only I'm no longer who I was, before.

Chore.

Falafel

I'm someone new. I don't know her yet.

I'm set.

Hungry, too.

I'm falling in love. With you.

Faith

I'm no longer angry. Afraid. Of what's next.

I must –

Trust

And so I must.

Trust.

Brooklyn

Baby

I'm building. Bridges.

I'm moving. Forward. Towards you.

Destiny

Child.

Survivor.

Self.

He

People ask, "were you always, a boy"? I say "no. I was, a toy".

I play, pretend. Another story.

Picture.

Art.

She

I was not. Always.

A boy.

I was a girl, before. Dresses, skirts.

Nerd

A lawyer.

Intellectual

Office, desk.

Documents, files.

Fire, flies.

Fortune.

> "You would not believe your eyes
> If ten million fireflies
> Lit up the world as I fell asleep
>
> Cause they'd fill the open air
> And leave teardrops everywhere
> You'd think me rude, but I would just stand and stare
>
> I'd like to make myself believe
> That planet Earth turns slowly
> It's hard to say that I'd rather stay awake when I'm asleep
> Cause everything is never as it seems"

Owl City

Stop

Take your time.

Rhyme.

Watch

And I surrender. It all.

To God. A bigger entity. The Universe.

With love.

Dove

And I work. My steps.

Five. Six, seven.

Heaven.

Reality

Show.

Deal

How do you feel?

I'm not feeling much, these days, I say.

I'm living. Giving.

Life.

Play

Pretend.

My voice is still high, my body soft. Curves. Bones.

Beautiful.

Androgyne

They say, you look like both.

A boy, girl.

Pearl.

People

Apologies.

Finally.

Fiction

Fantasy.

Stars

Dollars, money. Cash, will come in. At this point, it matters less.

It matters less what I'm doing, where I'm at.

I matter more. My friends, students. My clients, calls. My business.

Next to my writing, teaching. Art.

I'm running my life.

Finally.

Myself.

Cash

New York.

City.

I'm feeling better. Safer.

Sorry.

Glory

I finally have it. All.

Everything I ever dreamt of. A car, cash. Apartment, flat. Fame.

A garden. Terrace. Air.

Pyramids

They say, you must move forward.

Don't go back, stay. Present. Don't hide, surrender.

Serene.

Star.

Why

Do I care, so much?

Touch.

Nervous

My vows. A wedding.

Views.

Visions

Ceremony.

In ceremony, I see stars. Align.

Hurray

Is this progress?

Worry

My family.

Scenery

Arts.

LGBTQ. Centre.

Syllabus. How to. For dummies.

DNA.

Lavender

Boys kiss boys, girls. Girls kiss girls, boys. Back.

Stage.

Smoke

Playing, cards. Cigarettes.

A stroll, see sight.

I'm so lucky.

Star

And numbers, match.

I love it, when this happens.

Heaven

A match made in heaven.

And so it is.

Play

Write.

Playwright.

Worry

Money.

"Bring in the cash, honey."

Yoga

I still teach, play. Pretend.

At times, I open up. Other moments, classes, I'm calm. Serene.

Surrender.

Students

I love the people I'm working with. Against.

Another.

Story.

Impressionism. Flowers.

Music. Female.

Figures.

Quiet

My heart, a fresh.

Start.

Hit

This is it.

The right fit.

Medellin

I'm moving mountains.

And so it is.

Cusco

Did I see this coming?

No.

Did you?

Clothes

I'm not, a boy. I'm just messing. Playing, a game. Arts.

This is not real. Deal.

But what if it is? Real. Forever. What if this is my truth?

Dude.

Fame

Only if I'm true, I relate to you.

From the heart.

Art.

Earth

I'm here. Queer.

Movie

The less I move, the more I notice. I'm changing.

Every day.

Age

"It's okay", someone says. "Do not give up, just yet".

Getsemani

And I grow. Bigger, better. Faster, stronger.

Longer.

Work

"It works if you work it".

And so it is.

Outside

Tomboy.

/'tɑmˌbɔɪ/

"a girl who dresses and acts like a boy, esp.
in playing physical games that boys usually play"

My older brother. His name is Tom. It's a boy.

And so we're two. Tom. Boys.

We're 3.

A boy, girl, boy. Toy.

Time

Line.

Gitana

/dʒɪˈtɑːnə,

xiˈtana/

"a female Spanish gypsy"

"Gitana".

A luxury boutique.

Hotel.

Class

Continue.

Water

Wind.

Sunset, classes. Curiosity.

Clarity.

Coco

Only my body –

Nuts

I hate my body.

It's shape, size. It's essence.

Core. Femininity.

Deity.

Yoga

We practice.

Play.

People

Ask, say. What gender do you prefer?

A boy, I say. Shy.

And, what women do you fancy?

I don't, I say.

Know

I've never –

Never say never.

Ever.

Single

Sober.

Quiet.

Night.

A knight.

In shining armor.

"Amour".

Love.

Lady.

Boy

My lady story.

And so it is.

Celibacy

I focus. Do my job.

Work, play. Art.

Heart

Only I'm cold, at night.

Fearful, afraid.

Fights.

Fury

Early, morning.

Carrot, cake. I try to bake.

I fail, miserably. Why isn't someone else taking care of me?

Sofie

Only I'm no longer her.

Here. There.

Queer.

Late

I miss kind, gentle, smiles. Others.

Mothers.

Isolate

I hear you say.

"Just enjoy life, one day, at a time".

Rhyme.

Actress

I play, my part. I star, in my movie. Life.

Why wait for others if you can show up for yourself fully?

Emancipated, free. Enlightened, he. She.

We. Go, grow. Together.

They.

They

I'm not sure what words. To use.

"Choose", they say. "What pronoun do you prefer?"

> /ˈprəʊnaʊn/
> noun
>
> "a word that can function as a noun phrase used by itself and
> that refers either to the participants in the discourse
> (e.g. I, you) or to someone or something mentioned
> elsewhere in the discourse (e.g. she, it, this)."

They.

Pray

I lower my voice.

Tone, pitch.

"Witch".

Bitch

Boyfriend fit. Trousers.

Shirts.

Night

I start to dance. Clubs, music. Daylight.

Savings.

Fear

A lot.

Of fearful. Thoughts.

Feelings.

Calling

Boy. Girl.

"Puta".

They stare. Glare. Over my shoulders. Smile, when they see, my face.

It's a girl. Boy.

Both.

AA

Thank God.

I got. You.

Gay

Twenty four hours. A day.

Pray.

Clean

A day.

One day at a time, I pray.

Say

"I'm sorry.

Please forgive me. I love you.

Thank you."

Police

"Are you a boy or a girl?"

"Does it matter?"

Glass

Shatter.

A pub. Café, beer.

"Queer."

Knife

I'm running. For my life.

Get

Out. Of here.

Queer.

Anxiety

Xanax.

Weekend

I stay in bed. All day.

I pray.

What

At night, I wake up.

Worry.

Google

"Trans-"

"..."

Gender

Genius.

Birth

Transgender.

/tranzˈdʒɛndə
adjective

denoting or relating to a person whose sense of personal
identity and gender does not correspond with their birth sex
"a transgender activist and author"

Baby

Belly.

Button.

Water

Falls.

Uterus

Anxiety.

FTM

A first.

"short for female-to-male"

the books shed light on the lived experiences of FTMs in America

Man

What to do, see, say. I pray.

I'm terrified.

Worry

Is this my fault?

Did I cause this to happen? To me?

Sorry

"Forgive me father, for I have sinned".

Story

I did not sin.

I'm just finding my way. In my skin.

Body

New feelings emerge. Submerge.

Often.

Work

I can't move.

Anymore.

I stay still.

Chore.

Gym

Clothes.

Lose

Ends.

New

Beginnings.

Play

I try to enjoy my body.

It's not working yet.

Set

Let go, settle in.

Yourself.

Order

A new order.

Disorder.

Delay

Okay.

My lady story

"My lady story
My lady story

My lady story
Is one of annihilation
My lady story
Is one of breast amputation

My lady story
My lady story

I'm a hole in love
I'm a bride on fire
I am twisted
Into a starve of wire

My lady story
My lady story

Lie in road for you
And I've been your slave
My womb's an ocean full of
Grief and rage

My lady story
My lady story"

Antony and the Johnsons

My

Self.

I try to please, myself.

Masturbate, hate.

My body.

Love

Others. I don't feel.

Much.

Touch

And so I try. New.

Gay

Art.

Medellin

I feel better here. Queer.

Open, wide. Night. Life, lovers.

Sebastian opens. My door.

Room for more.

Tea

A friend, not yet. Maybe.

Do you see?

Ayahuasca

Guitar. Strings.

"This is the place for all my relations
To bring celebration through meditation
Giving thanks for all of creation
We are so provided for
We are so provided for
We are so provided for
We are so provided for"

Mitakuye Oyasin

Retreat

Few days later, I arrive. At my new job, retreat center.

I still love teaching. Yoga.

My students.

High

Up here, mountain. Climate.

Carmen.

Viboral

I'm cold. Often.

My sweater, shirts.

Do not cover up my body. Chilly.

Say

"Hey, have you got a sweater?"

I do, she says. A girl, size. Sweater.

Storm.

Yes

I say "Thank you", try it on.

Take it off.

Girl

I just can't –

I'd rather be cold.

Students

Sit, still. Quiet.

A wooden *shala*.

And so we practice.

Pray.

Students

Play.

I'm in the midst of it.

We're in the midst of it.

What

This.

That.

All of it, really.

All of it.

Everything.

Sing

I play.

A song, Samantha sings.

Pocahontas.

A picture.

Drawing.

Art.

Dress

On my desk. Bedside. "Girl".

Only I'm not. A girl.

Pearl

A safe. Harbor.

Storm.

Bogota

Villa de Leyva

Alibies.

Allies.

/ˈalʌɪ/

a state formally cooperating with another for a military or
other purpose
"debate continued among NATO allies"

Alert

Advisor.

Via

"Sofia."

A door, mat.

Reply

I refuse, resist.

"I'm not sure yet".

I forget.

Fit

Am I losing it? Or did I find it.

None of it. It just is.

What it is.

Today

And so I pray.

Starbucks

I'll go to New York.

One day.

Coffee

"Hi", I say.

"Simon".

"Yes".

Espejo

Cry, my eyes.

Out

Come.

Cool

"Pray to catch you whispering
I pray you catch me listening
I'm praying to catch you whispering
I pray you catch me
I'm praying to catch you whispering
I pray you catch me listening
I pray you catch me"

Beyonce

Dishonesty

I'm praying for a different outcome.

Anything but this.

Cis

Gender.

/sɪsˈdʒɛndə/

denoting or relating to a person whose sense of personal identity and gender corresponds with their birth sex

"this new-found attention to the plight of black trans folks by primarily cisgender allies is timely and necessary"

Christmas

Tree.

I try to be, but I'm not.

Gender

Genes.

Girl

But I prefer to be a boy. Toy.

Art.

Arts

Charity.

Toy, tools. Therapy.

I'll get there.

Here.

I'm here.

Queer.

And so it is.

Clarity

Dignity.

Culture

What name, do you prefer?

I'm silent.

"Simon", I say. Pray.

Queer

And Charly, too.

Simon Charly.

And so it is.

New

York.

City

Open.

Doors.

ABC

All night long.

                              DJ

My song.

House

Yes.

God bless.

It's just –

Chess

A game.

Over.

Other

Story.

Balls

Glory.

God

Guru.

Spirit

Guides.

Generation

Queer.

Dear

"One day I'll grow up, I'll be a beautiful woman
One day I'll grow up, I'll be a beautiful girl
One day I'll grow up, I'll be a beautiful woman
One day I'll grow up, I'll be a beautiful girl

But for today I am a child, for today I am a boy
For today I am a child, for today I am a boy
For today I am a child, for today I am a boy

One day I'll grow up, I'll feel the power in me
One day I'll grow up, of this I'm sure
One day I'll grow up, I know whom within me
One day I'll grow up, feel it full and pure

But for today I am a child, for today I am a boy
For today I am a child, for today I am a boy
For today I am a child, for today I am a boy"

Antony and the Johnsons

www.ingramcontent.com/pod-product-compliance
Lightning Source LLC
Chambersburg PA
CBHW021810170526
45157CB00007B/2532